Timeshare Truths

Navigate Pitfalls and Unveil Hidden Costs

10 Essential Questions for Secure Informed Investments

Freeman Publishing

Table of Contents

Introduction

The good news is that you can enjoy luxurious holidays and vacations without having to pay expensive seasonal rates. It is possible you have heard negative comments about purchasing timeshares. You may be unsure about how to proceed to be sure you have a hassle-free timeshare buying process. Review this concise guide before attending high-pressure timeshare presentations. Avoid a negative experience and buyer's remorse.

This book will address 10 questions that every buyer should answer before buying a timeshare. For example, you may not know the answer to "What is a timeshare?" Most importantly, you will find out what your rights are regarding timeshare purchases. The 10 questions this pocket-sized guide answers are enough to gain the necessary confidence when making the long-term commitment to a timeshare.

Whether you're looking for information on how timeshares work, how to finance their purchase, why it's necessary to pay maintenance fees, or what your rights are, this guide is there for you.

You will also learn about questionable tactics that some timeshare professionals use to try and sell you their vacation properties.

Many timeshare owners don't always consider what they will do with their timeshare in the future or if they are disappointed because their purchase fails to meet their expectations. This guide points out considerations that will better prepare you for time-share ownership. If this sounds good, let's get started with the first chapter.

Chapter 1

Timeshare Properties 101

A timeshare contract is like a marriage contract. It has no end date, and you don't know how much it's going to cost you.

A rule of thumb about investments is, if you sign a contract make sure there is an exit clause.

With this in mind, what are your options if you no longer want to travel or use your timeshare? What happens if you can't afford uncontrolled, ongoing timeshare-related costs? Answers to these questions and others are crucial before entering into a binding timeshare contract.

I recommend hiring a real estate attorney to review your timeshare contract before you sign it or soon after signing it but before the grace period expires. It is definitely worth spending a couple of hundred dollars to have a qualified real estate attorney review the contract to safeguard the tens of thousands of dollars you are committing to.

We begin with the fundamentals of timeshares. In this chapter, we cover what a timeshare is, how it works, and the different types of timeshares.

What Is a Timeshare Property?

Owning a vacation home is great if you enjoy taking regular holidays. Two of the most important factors to consider when buying a vacation home are cost and location. If this concerns you and you still want to take regular vacations, one option is a *timeshare*: a vacation property in which you share the costs of ownership or leasing with others. Note that *fractional ownership* refers to luxurious vacation properties available for part ownership and usage of more than one week.

There are different structures for timeshare property ownership. The specific terms of your contract determine the nature of ownership as well as your usage rights.

You will have either a shared deeded contract or a shared right-to-use, leased contract.

- Shared deeded contract: This type of contract gives you a certain ownership percentage of the physical property. Buying a shared deeded ownership is like purchasing a home. You typically purchase a specific week or set of weeks that you're allowed to use the property. If you purchase one week in a year, your ownership percentage of the timeshare is 1.92% (1/52 x 100 = 1.92%).

A shared deeded contract confers perpetual ownership; it can be gifted, sold, or bequeathed.

- Shared right-to-use contract: With this type of contract, you have the right to use a timeshare unit for a fixed or floating week annually for a certain number of years. You have no right to sell, gift, or transfer your ownership.

The timeshare developer retains ownership of the property.

The main difference between the above contract options is that a shared deeded contract gives you property ownership, while a shared lease contract does not. Because of this distinction, the pricing of similar timeshare units in the same location will differ.

How Does the Ownership Structure Work?

When you consider buying or leasing a timeshare, there is more to consider than the type of contract. One of those factors is the ownership structure. This knowledge can help you make an informed decision.

- Fixed week timeshare: This is timeshare ownership at a vacation property during a given week of the year. If you're allocated week #49 of the year, you will use the property only during that period. A fixed week timeshare usually employs a shared deeded contract. It's a great option when you have fixed vacation periods such as school holidays or anniversaries. The pros are that you have a guaranteed vacation home, it allows easy hosting of family, and you don't need too much planning ahead. However, it offers no flexibility—the same resort on the same dates every year means your vacation time is rigid.

- Floating week timeshare: You have the right to use a timeshare unit during any predefined season. Usage of the property can vary from one year to the next. You have to contact your resort each year when you want to reserve a unit at the resort during a given season. Seasons vary from one resort to another and can range from weeks 1–52, 17–24, or any other range. Pros include allowing you to visit based on family commitments and lifestyle, and they may have higher availability than the fixed week versions. The cons to consider include the possibility of price increases that can be difficult to upkeep, and you're not allowed to rent out the property to third parties.
- Fractional ownership structure: This ownership model is the same as that of a fixed week timeshare. The difference is that with a fractional timeshare, you, most likely, have the right to use the property for longer than a week, such as four weeks per year. It tends to be luxurious and a standalone property such as a condo or standalone home. The pros are that it has fewer owners, your ownership portion can be sold or handed over to another person, and its value mimics market trends. However, it can be pricier to purchase, has higher annual fees, and may be challenging to sell.
- Points ownership structure: This is a structure in which you purchase a number of points within a vacation club membership to be used to stay in a property within the club. The demand for unit sizes and vacation dates at each resort determines the number of points you pay. You can own a single-destination or multi-destination timeshare. The pros include flexibility in terms of unit sizes, vacation dates, and duration, in addition to the ability to choose between multiple resorts and the

rollover of points. The cons to consider include the need to plan ahead, lack of availability during peak seasons, and the inability to reserve outside designated times.

- Biennial ownership structure: Here you have the right to use your timeshare ownership every other year, which is why this model is also called EOY usage. Your biennial ownership contract specifies either Even or Odd Years when you will have access to the property. Biennial ownership tends to be cheaper and could be ideal if you have less paid time off at your job, giving you more time to accumulate sufficient vacation time when it's your year. However, it's nearly impossible to change vacation years, and the model lacks flexibility in terms of location.

In a nutshell, a timeshare is a part ownership property model that allows you to enjoy your vacations without buying an entire vacation home. Various ownership structures present travel options that suit your needs. For instance, you can purchase a deeded or non-deeded fixed or floating week. If you prefer a luxurious vacation property, considering fractional ownership may be your best bet. A $^1/_8$ ownership of a mansion in the vineyards of Napa Valley currently sells for about $500,000.

There is more to consider before purchasing a timeshare, including cost and location. The next chapter dives into the location factor.

Notes

____

____

Chapter 2

Location, Location, Location!

There are 1,541 timeshare resorts and 201,600 units in the US, which is an average of 131 units per resort (ARDA, n.d.). With this substantial number of timeshare properties to choose from, it can be difficult to decide which one would be best for you. When you're finished reading this chapter, you will know the best way to select a desirable timeshare.

How Do I Decide on the Best Location for My Timeshare Purchase?

Now that you know the different timeshare ownership structures, it's time to figure out where to buy your timeshare. When thinking about this, the first key decision to make is not the kind of property you want but the exact location of the timeshare.

Before choosing a location, ask yourself these two questions: "Do I love going to a specific vacation spot every year?" or "Do I prefer to visit new places sometimes when I take a vacation?" If going to the same location resonates with you and your family, it's crucial to choose a place you will enjoy vacationing for many years or decades to come.

However, if you prefer switching up vacation locations, consider evaluating the pros and cons of a single-destination timeshare against the timeshare trade or exchange option. Buying a timeshare for its trade or exchange value offers the flexibility you don't have with single-destination timeshares. With the ability to trade or exchange, you should have access to a larger selection of vacation resorts and destinations. This flexibility comes with extra costs, such as exchange fees and the real possibility of the inability to trade for a timeshare you desire due to lack of availability.

Furthermore, buying a specific location, like Orlando, can offer flexibility if you have a floating week contract. This comes in handy if you need to adjust vacation dates due to factors such as work schedules or changing school holidays. High usage periods like Easter, Spring break, Thanksgiving, Christmas, and other holidays can be difficult to exchange into if you own a less desirable location.

For high location flexibility, the most preferred timeshare ownership structure is the points system. You purchase a set number of points when you buy your timeshare. Often, you are given a range of points to choose from at a set price per point. These points can be used to travel to any resort within the developer's resort collection. The number of points required for a particular property varies by day, date, weekends vs weekdays, type of unit, number of bedrooms, etc.

Here are some important tips to consider when choosing a timeshare location:

- Physically Inspect Your Potential Timeshare: Personally visit and inspect the prospective timeshare resort and its location. This is like the home inspection you conduct when buying a personal home. Check for family fit, condition, amenities, and scenery to ensure the unit meets your expectations before making a commitment.
- Evaluate accommodations and amenities: Timeshares are classified based on the quality of their accommodations and amenities, such as access to gyms, pools, or golf courses. Your choice will depend on your budget and preferences. If you want high-end resort-level amenities, consider timeshares that feel like a home. In contrast, luxurious timeshares that offer perks like car rentals typically have the Interval International (II) award or the Resort Condominiums International (RCI) Gold Crown.
- Understand the limitations of salespeople: Note that the timeshare sales representatives are not involved in exchange requests and may not be aware of the availability or scarcity of the properties you desire. Exchange requests are handled by third-party companies like RCI and II. If a salesperson assures you that you can effortlessly exchange your particular timeshare for many desirable locations, be aware that many variables go into exchange requests. Ask yourself these questions: "Is it better to purchase at the most desirable location?" or "Should I keep my home resort if I'm happy with vacationing there frequently, as well as having possible access to desirable properties through an external exchange program?"

There are multiple timeshare contract options and their associated locations. It's ultimately your call regarding the location you desire and the kind of timeshare. Carefully consider how often you want to visit a particular location as opposed to traveling domestically or internationally.

How Flexible Is the Exchange Program?

A *timeshare exchange program* offers you the ability to trade or exchange your timeshare for another. You can do this within your vacation club or externally with II or RCI.

Internal exchanges: These allow you to trade or exchange your timeshare with a comparable unit within the same vacation club or resort, providing more travel flexibility while enjoying similar benefits offered by a particular developer.

External exchanges: These provide timeshare owners with the opportunity to trade-in their properties and travel to a different location or resort within the exchange company. They are commonly offered by third-party exchange companies such as RCI and II (Interval International). To exchange your timeshare, simply deposit your points or week by a designated time each year then submit your request when you have chosen from the alternatives available.

Note that you may not get the kind of timeshare you want due to factors such as location, type, demand, and the exchange popularity of your own resort.

Most importantly, familiarize yourself with the requirements of the associated timeshare exchange companies and vacation club rules, in addition to membership fees for the exchange company and applicable exchange fees.

Navigating Timeshare Exchanges

It can be tricky to find a desirable exchange. You need a thorough strategy and plan to avoid falling into the trap of trading down to a less-than-desirable option. Here are some of the steps you can take to get the timeshare you want:

- Plan far in advance and book at least nine months ahead to secure a high-demand timeshare. Some exchange companies have limits on when your window of opportunity is to make your exchange request. You need to know this. If you are not allowed to make a request more than 90 days out, the availability at a desirable location may be greatly reduced.
- Research the resort you want to request and the timeshare exchange company rules before you consider making a booking to know what the likelihood is of getting what you want. There may be specific regulations regarding timeshare exchange programs in some states, highlighting the importance of researching before purchasing.
- Ask the name of the exchange company's contact when making exchange requests and research any complaints against the exchange company prior to buying a timeshare that locks you in to a specific exchange company.

Some third-party exchange companies have tools such as deposit calculators or wait lists to help you as you research and choose exchange timeshares. Keep in mind that the availability of exchange timeshares depends on supply and demand. This can make it challenging to trade your timeshare during busy seasons. Also remember, the exchange companies operate independently of the timeshare resort properties and will not be able to give you information about other resorts other than their availability during the time period you indicate and exchange-related information such as size of unit and fees.

Some of the most sought-after timeshares in the US include the following:

- Club Wyndham: Wyndham owns Shell Vacations Club with its small collection of resorts, as well as the exchange company RCI, and offers a vast number of options, including Las Vegas, Hawaii, Orlando, Miami, Colorado, New York City, San Diego, San Francisco, and Washington DC.
- Hyatt Residence Club: The club allows you to borrow or bank your points and use them at any Hyatt resort.
- Disney Vacation Club: Disney offers a unique vacation experience and perks such as owner-only events and pool hopping.
- Hilton Grand Vacations Club: HGV auto-enrolls you into the Hilton Honors program for extra benefits such as extended holiday stays. Because it's affiliated with RCI, you can access thousands of exchange timeshares for enhanced flexibility.

The choice of whether or where to purchase a timeshare property depends on your traveling habits. If you prefer a vacation at the same place each year, a deeded week—fixed or floating—could be the way to go. On the other hand, the points system will be ideal if you seek travel variety. You can also enjoy multi-destination traveling through a timeshare exchange company. In addition to the adage of "Location, location, location" and your travel preferences, you need to be aware of timeshare costs other than the purchase price that are detailed in the next chapter.

Notes

Chapter 3

Let's Talk About Money

A one week vacation in the US costs an average of $1,578 per person (Bennett, 2022). If you go on vacation with another person, double that for a total of $3,156. When you consider that you may be traveling with children and other family members, your vacation costs could quickly jump into serious money.

What if you opted to purchase a timeshare? In 2022, you would have needed to fork out approximately $24,140 for a one week ownership stake in a timeshare property (Araj, 2022). Does this amount sound affordable? Before you answer this question, let's dig deeper into the costs of owning a timeshare.

How Much Is This Going to Cost Me?

It costs money upfront to own a timeshare. This includes the one-time purchase fee, current year's maintenance fees, possible special assessments, closing costs, transfer fees, and taxes. Let's briefly look into each of these costs:

- One-time purchase fee: This is the overall purchase price of a timeshare that may be the same as its listed price. It can range anywhere from $10,000–$100,000, subject to variables such as size, ownership structure, and location (Centerstone Group, n.d.). For a $24,140 timeshare, you will need to use it nearly 16 times ($24,140/$1,578 = 15.3) to recoup just the initial cost (not including annual maintenance fees).
- Annual maintenance fees: Ownership of a timeshare comes with maintenance costs, just as with any residential property. I will go into more detail about these costs in the next section.
- Special assessments: These are the costs to cover damage due to unforeseen events such as flooding, earthquakes, or hurricanes—events not usually covered by basic insurance policies.
- Other costs: These include closing costs, taxes, title, and transfer fees normally included in real estate transactions.

As mentioned briefly above, there are important factors that drive timeshare costs. Other than size and location, how much you pay will depend on where you make the purchase of the timeshare. If you purchase from the resort sales group after the presentation, you're likely to pay more than if you bought a similar property in the resale market.

Branding also carries weight. For example, a Marriott Vacation Club timeshare's cost will be different from a Disney Vacation Club timeshare. The reason for this is that the quality of amenities also comes into play, as does the popularity of the resort and availability.

When deciding to purchase a timeshare, keep in mind that its value rarely appreciates over time. It, therefore, should be considered a luxury purchase rather than a real estate investment. This calls for thorough research to get value for the timeshare you purchase.

Finance Options for Your Timeshare

You don't need cash upfront to pay for your timeshare, as financing is available. Some options include the following:

- Home equity loan: If you have been paying your mortgage for a couple of years, you may have built up equity in your home. Borrowing against that equity may provide the funds to purchase a timeshare at lower interest rates compared to taking a personal loan. Remember that a home equity loan could result in the foreclosure of your home and timeshare if you default on payments.
- Credit card: This option tends to come with high interest rates, but you can sometimes find 0% annual percentage rate (APR) promotional offers for up to 18 months. If you can pay off your down payment within this period, it could be an attractive option. However, you will need to pay off the balance before the promotional offer expires to avoid paying extremely high interest rates.
- Personal loan: This can be a viable option if you have a strong credit score. The interest rates may be lower than those being offered by timeshare sales agents but higher than for home equity loans because they are unsecured.
- Timeshare loans: Developers offer these to help make funding accessible and more manageable. These are

faster to secure because lenders usually work with the timeshare sales team. Repayment terms tend to be longer, which leads to lower installment payments. The biggest drawback is that they often have high interest rates and additional costs.

From the upfront purchasing cost perspective, a timeshare is cheaper than renting a vacation home. You can pay an average of $292 per day and up to $791 a day, depending on factors such as location (Jade, 2022). If you rent a vacation home for one week, you can pay as much as $5,537 ($791 x 7 = $5,537). Buying a timeshare also includes covering long-term maintenance costs, making it necessary to include that factor when you make comparisons with renting a vacation home like Airbnb.

In the next chapter, we'll delve into the often-overlooked expenses associated with timeshare ownership, ensuring you're armed with a holistic financial perspective before making your decision.

What About Maintenance?

Much like owning a house or condo, owning a timeshare comes with its own set of obligatory expenses—notably, the annual maintenance fees.

Think of these costs like the Homeowners Association (HOA) fees that owners pay for the upkeep of a community's common areas. Every timeshare owner pays a certain amount of money annually to cover labor expenses for the upkeep of the property, utilities, insurance, amenities, and any upgrades to the property. The total maintenance costs are divided among the timeshare owners.

The maintenance fee you pay varies based on factors such as the location of your timeshare and unit size. On average, you can expect to be charged $1,000+ in annual maintenance fees and more in subsequent years due to yearly increases (Araj, 2022). These fees vary from one developer to the next, but you will know when you receive your bill between August and November for fees for the next calendar year. Payments are usually due by January 1. Your contract will specify not only how much to pay and the frequency but also the rate of annual increases. Defaulting on these payments can jeopardize access to your unit, and access to any exchange programs could be affected.

Can you deduct your maintenance fees for tax purposes? Generally, you cannot, the same as for your own home regarding home improvement costs. However, you could possibly deduct them if you own the timeshare in a legal entity such as a limited liability company (LLC). For a customized answer to this question, you should consult a tax professional who is knowledgeable about timeshare ownership.

You might have come across dubious claims suggesting that halting maintenance fee payments is a pathway to terminating your timeshare contract. Questions like this arise because some scam timeshare-cancellation companies erroneously advise owners who want to cancel their timeshare ownership contracts to stop paying maintenance fees. Owning a timeshare is similar to other real estate ownership. If you don't pay the contractual fees as agreed, you put your credit history at risk.

As part of your research, evaluate how well the developer maintains their properties. It's a good idea to find out the name of the management company and check their track record. Search online for reviews, complaints, and pending legal issues.

In summary, owning a timeshare tends to be cheaper than buying a vacation home; you just need to make sure you can afford ongoing costs. If you don't have the cash to pay for the price of the timeshare, you have options such as a credit card, personal loan, timeshare loan, or home equity loan. When calculating the cost of your timeshare, you should include any interest paid as part of the cost of this investment. Make sure you regularly pay maintenance fees to protect your credit record.

Before you make a commitment to purchase a timeshare, it's worth understanding your rights and the rules and regulations that govern timeshares. We will review these in the next chapter.

Notes

Chapter 4

Rights, Rules, and Regulations

The timeshare industry adds $73.1 billion to the US economy, with $10.7 billion in tax revenue and $29.3 billion in income and wages. For comparison, Major League Basketball and the recorded music industry each contribute less than one-seventh the size of the timeshare sector (ARDA, n.d.). As an important sector of the US economy, the timeshare industry is bound to be regulated. This is good news because you have certain rights, as discussed below.

What Are My Usage Rights, and How Do Legal Regulations Vary by State?

Timeshare developers and operators must comply with state laws. The contract you sign confers certain rights to you and complies with that state's laws. Your timeshare usage rights depend entirely upon the contract. In light of this, there are some aspects to check, such as whether there are restrictions on usage by season and how far in advance you can make reservations. Make sure that you read the contract to fully understand your rights and that you comply with your responsibilities.

Why Timeshare Laws Vary by State

There is no US federal law that governs the sale of timeshares, which leaves each state to create its own laws. The number of timeshares in each state varies greatly, which is one reason some states have strict timeshare laws while others have more relaxed laws. Having stricter laws may be a good thing, as that may give timeshare owners greater protection.

Some states, such as California, belong to the group of states having tougher or more restrictive timeshare laws. For instance, they stipulate what every purchase contract must include. California stipulates that you should be furnished with a disclosure document before you sign the timeshare contract. Anytime material upgrades are made to the resort, this report must be updated.

States such as Florida and Nevada have more relaxed timeshare laws. The developer must also make sure that their purchase contract complies with consumer protection requirements.

As a timeshare buyer, you don't have to worry about registering the timeshare plan or obtaining the permit to sell/buy. It's the developer's job to apply and obtain the state permit to sell to you. To register the timeshare plan, the developer follows these steps:

1. Applying for registration: This may vary by state, and the application should include financial information and the organizational structure of the developer, as well as zoning compliance documents.
2. Issuing the disclosure document: The developer is mandated to provide every prospective buyer with the disclosure document before signing the contract. The

disclosure document contains details such as use restrictions, description of the accommodation, type of timeshare plan, and property information.

3. Reviewing the application: The state reviews the application to make sure it's complete. If it finds deficiencies, it issues a deficiency notice to the developer to correct whatever is inaccurate or include anything that is missing. States like Nevada and California have 60–120 days to review the developer's application, depending on the size of the property. Some states, like California, may also issue preliminary permits for the developer to complete a limited set of activities. (Spaulding Jr. et al., 2022)

Certain states may require developers to open escrow accounts into which they place buyers' funds during the so-called cooling-off, grace, or recission period. When this period passes, the developer may withdraw those funds. This is important for buyers to know because they can have peace of mind during the initial period when buying a timeshare in case they change their mind within the allotted grace period.

Timeshares can be foreclosed the same way as homes. Common causes of timeshare foreclosures include defaulting on maintenance fees, special assessments, utilities, or taxes. The laws governing foreclosure vary by state. If you think you can sell your timeshare to avoid foreclosure, you still need to comply with the resale regulations in place and may vary from state to state.

One crucial element of purchasing a timeshare is understanding fraud and misrepresentation by timeshare salespeople. Developers might use a practice called fraudulent inducement to get you to buy a timeshare. If this happens to you, it is crucial to know how to prove this misrepresentation. For example, you will need to prove that the developer made a specific false representation. Again, this emphasizes the importance of understanding the process of buying a timeshare and your associated rights.

What Is the Cooling-off Period, and How Can I Cancel My Contract?

Buyer's remorse is a real thing in life. You commit to buying a timeshare, and the next day, you feel you may have made the wrong decision. In such a case, could you rescind your purchase decision? You absolutely can, irrespective of the state involved, because most states specify what is known as the rescission, cooling-off period, or grace period.

A *recission*, *cooling-off period*, or *grace period* is the number of days you're given to cancel a timeshare contract without penalty. Most states give you between 3 and 15 days to rescind your timeshare contract after you have signed it. For instance, in Florida, you have a ten-day window, while California and Nevada give you 5 calendar days to cancel your timeshare contract, as does Colorado. Your fifth day ends at midnight. Bear in mind laws change and the grace period varies by state, meaning you should absolutely check to see exactly what the recission period is in the state the timeshare is being purchased.

The law gives you the right to cancel your contract orally. However, sending your cancellation in writing is recommended because you will then have written documentation. Your cancellation letter should include the following:

- current date/time and reference to the grace period
- your personal details, such as your name, address, email address, and phone number

- the timeshare details, including the timeshare company, timeshare purchase date, and description of the timeshare as stated in your contract
- a statement that clearly describes your intention to cancel the contract

Make sure you include everything delineated in your state law concerning the cancellation of a timeshare contract. Check to see how you should send your cancellation notice. Whatever delivery method you're required to use, ensure that your letter reaches your timeshare company within the stated grace period/cancellation period.

If you bought a timeshare in a foreign country, the laws of that country prevail and will guide you about the cancellation period and requirements.

One of the questions timeshare buyers often ask is whether they can cancel their timeshare contracts after the expiration of the rescission period. In many instances, it may be close to impossible to cancel or dispose of your timeshare without taking a significant loss. Your best bet will be to try and sell it in the resale market. As explained earlier, be careful when you are selling your timeshare in the secondary market. Beware of companies offering to sell your timeshare for a fee without giving you a timeline or guarantee.

Summary

While offering a unique vacationing experience, timeshares come with a strict set of rules, regulations, and responsibilities. As a potential buyer, it's paramount that you acquaint yourself with the nuances of the timeshare laws in the state of purchase.

You should buy a timeshare only after you understand your rights. It would be imprudent to sign a timeshare contract without knowing about the cancellation period and process and all of the rules surrounding its disposal. Hire an attorney or read the disclosure document and purchase contract thoroughly before putting pen to paper. Most importantly, avoid buying a timeshare until you have thought about the future.

In the next chapter, we delve into some common myths and misconceptions about timeshares, helping you to discern fact from fiction in the world of timeshare ownership.

Notes

Chapter 5

Thinking About the Future

What if I told you that it's possible you might only be able to get $1 for your timeshare when you sell it? Yes, bids on timeshare properties listed on classified ad websites like Craigslist and eBay can start as low as $1 (Why Timeshares Lose Value, n.d.). It would be tragic if you bought your timeshare for tens of thousands of dollars and paid escalating maintenance fees for decades only to receive $1 once you are no longer able to take advantage of this asset. What this means is that you could lose a significant amount of money on a timeshare purchase, making it absolutely necessary to do your homework prior to committing. This chapter covers some of the long-term aspects to consider before you sign on the dotted line.

What Are the Rules for Resale?

Remember, as we mentioned earlier, if you sign a contract make sure there is an exit clause.

It would be extremely poor planning to purchase a timeshare without an exit strategy. If your exit strategy is to simply resell, you should understand what is involved before putting pen to paper. Not only will this give you peace of mind, but it can also save you a significant amount of money in the long run.

The one question you should have an unequivocal answer to is who will buy your timeshare? Looking into the resale market will quickly show you whether it's possible to resell your timeshare and for how much.

In summary, it's essential to understand how to dispose of your timeshare if you should want to.

Selling Your Timeshare

The first key action to take is to review your contract and all paperwork related to your timeshare ownership. Check the details of the timeshare, including its physical location, developer's name, amenities, size, and description. Confirm who holds the title to the timeshare, whether it's a deeded or non-deeded contract. Review the kind of access to the property you have.

The next step is to research the value of your timeshare. As mentioned earlier, you should not expect to make more than you paid for the timeshare because its value is unlikely to increase over time. Timeshares are like cars in that their value usually declines as time passes. Thus, it's a good idea to focus on optimizing the amount of money you can get from the sale. Also, verify that you have paid off the timeshare sales contract and that you are up to date regarding ongoing expenses. Check websites such as eBay, Users Group, Redweek.com, and Craigslist to see how much similar timeshares are selling for in your location.

Once you have completed the above research, it's time to decide whether to sell your timeshare yourself, use an agent, or hire a resale company. If you don't have the expertise to sell timeshares, it's a good idea to hire an experienced timeshare agent or a resale company. Only consider reputable resale companies that belong to groups such as the ARDA and the Better Business Bureau to avoid being scammed.

You may fail to sell your timeshare through the above-mentioned avenues. If that happens, check with your timeshare's resort management office to see if they can help dispose of your ownership interest or just take it back and cancel your future obligations.

The timeshare resale industry is rife with questionable conduct. Some of the red flags to watch for include:

- Advice to stop paying ongoing fees: Do not do this. Not paying legally obligated costs like maintenance fees may obstruct your ability to resell your timeshare and damage your credit record.
- Massive upfront fees: Any company demanding thousands of dollars in upfront, nonrefundable fees should provide a written guarantee of the sale.
- Cold calls, phone messages, or texts promising there is an interested buyer for your timeshare: Resale companies may do this randomly. Unless you have given them permission to contact you for that purpose, don't entertain them.
- No-guarantee promises to cancel your contract: It is not easy to cancel a timeshare contract once the recission

period has lapsed. Your contract will stipulate if you can do this and how to go about doing so.

- Upfront fees to exit lawyers or teams: Treat these companies and lawyers the same way I have suggested above about cancellation services. Be sure to have a written guarantee that they can cancel your timeshare contract before you pay a fee. It is still your responsibility to make sure you interact with reputable exit companies and attorneys.

Can You Inherit a Timeshare?

The short answer is that timeshares can be inherited whether they are held in perpetuity or for a fixed period.

It is crucial to consider the disposition of your timeshare after death.

Timeshares are treated like all other assets of a deceased person. Whether you want to inherit one or not is not an easy decision to make. After all, there are many factors to bear in mind, such as ongoing annual fees and your personal lifestyle.

A timeshare purchase may be in perpetuity or for a fixed period. A timeshare owned in perpetuity means you own the title forever. To ensure that your heir gets it, you will need to name them as a co-trustee. The timeshare inheritor has three options: They can keep it, sell it, or abandon it.

- Keeping it: Heirs might appreciate receiving your timeshare if the inheritor loves traveling and has the money to do so each year. Additionally, if the purchase contract is not fully paid off, the inheritor would typically be responsible for these debts. However, laws vary by state, and in some cases, the inheritor might not be legally obligated to take on the deceased's debt. Recognize that the inheritor will need to be able to cover ongoing maintenance fees and other outstanding costs.

- Tax implications: Just like other inherited property, timeshares can have tax implications. Depending on the state tax laws where the timeshare is located, the inheritor might be responsible for paying the inheritance tax. Consult a tax professional to understand the potential obligations or benefits.
- Selling or renting it: The inheritor who does not have the cash to travel or pay maintenance fees for the timeshare may choose to sell it, give it away to someone else, or rent it. Selling it involves the same steps listed above when we discussed reselling options. Alternatively, the inheritor may rent out their timeshare, putting some cash in their pockets in the year they are not using it.
- Abandoning it: The inheritor who does not want to be obligated to the costs of keeping the timeshare may abandon it. All it takes is crafting a Disclaimer of Interest to inform the developer and other interested parties that you refuse the inheritance and do not want to keep the timeshare. To submit this document, you will be required to pay a fee to free yourself of the timeshare obligations.

During your estate planning, be sure you understand the following:

- Probate: Your timeshare may be subject to probate, a time-consuming and possibly challenging process for your heirs. During this period, your heirs will not be able to use the timeshare, but your estate continues to be obligated to pay fees for maintenance and other applicable costs.

- Naming a co-trustee: This comes in handy when an heir intends to sell your timeshare. Naming your beneficiary as the co-trustee gives them the right to decide what to do with the timeshare. The big advantage of naming a co-trustee is that your estate will not have to pay ongoing fees after your death. Be sure to verify this with your contract details or an attorney.
- Trust: Putting your timeshare in a revocable living trust is one of the best ways to avoid probate and enjoy possible tax benefits. Your heirs will know what to do with the timeshare because there will be explicit instructions about transferring it when you are gone.
- Joint tenants: Titling your timeshare as joint tenants can temporarily put the brakes on probate. When you pass away, the title will pass to the person you hold the title with, such as your spouse. Probate will only kick in when this person dies.

In light of the aforementioned, if you want your heirs to have more control over the timeshare and protect it when you die, consider adding it to a revocable trust or titling it as joint tenants.

It's crucial to check the timeshare contract to establish if it contains a perpetuity clause or not. This will give you an idea regarding how to treat it in your estate plan. If you inherit a timeshare, remember that you will be charged with the responsibilities associated with owning it. Be sure to thoroughly evaluate all personal and financial implications before deciding how to proceed.

Summary

If your exit strategy is selling your timeshare, do your homework before proceeding. Understand the existing situation of your timeshare, including all associated costs. You can sell your timeshare yourself, but it may be better to hire a resale company or an agent who specializes in timeshare resales and has a proven track record. Alternatively, you can pass on your timeshare to your heirs by naming a co-trustee, titling your timeshare as joint tenants, or putting your timeshare in a revocable living trust.

Notes

Conclusion

A large purchase such as a timeshare should not be made impulsively. Such a commitment requires thorough knowledge, which, in turn, necessitates doing some pre-purchase homework. This book has provided the foundation you need to perform proper research.

Let's quickly review the important points.

You first learned that a timeshare is a part ownership of a vacation property. The big advantage is that you spend a fraction of the amount of money you would pay for a single-owner house, condo, townhouse, or apartment vacation property. Buying a timeshare gives you the right to use it during certain periods of the year. However, the question of when you can use it depends on the type of timeshare you purchase—for example, a fixed vs a floating week.

One of the most important factors that goes into the timeshare buying decision is location. If you travel at fixed periods during the year, a fixed week timeshare is your best bet. Otherwise, consider purchasing a floating week contract or one with the ability to exchange with other timeshares. Your final decision will depend on your financial situation and traveling habits.

When you have made up your mind that you want to purchase, there are important factors to consider. One of them is the purchase price and ongoing costs for keeping the timeshare. Purchase prices vary depending on location, size of the timeshare, and amenities and can go up to $100,000. You also need to contribute toward the maintenance of the resort or complex. This fee is currently around $1,000 annually for a basic one week purchase at an average resort property. Maintenance costs may increase each year. Similar to making any large purchase, you can finance your timeshare purchase with options such as home equity loans, credit cards, personal loans, or loans from the timeshare developer. Make sure you can afford whichever financing method you opt for.

Another crucial aspect to be sure of before you buy a timeshare is understanding your rights as an owner. A key document to study closely before making a buying decision is the purchase contract. Understand that this document may vary from state to state. Whichever state you are considering, find out what recission or cooling-off period you have and your rights and requirements for canceling the contract once you have signed it.

There's a powerful rule to consider before making any investment or purchasing any real estate property. You must have an exit strategy; this also applies to the purchase of the timeshare. If you're going to resell it, it's crucial to understand the timeshare secondary market. Be aware of questionable practices of exit companies and lawyers, such as advising you to stop paying maintenance fees. Also, consider best practices when you include your timeshare in your estate.

Having said that, buying a timeshare can be a good decision for you and your family. If you are fond of traveling and have the means to make this purchase, a carefully thought-out investment strategy can mean decades of family fun. It might, for instance, reduce the upfront vacation planning costs, may be exchanged if your vacation club allows, and can give you the opportunity to travel where you want when you want.

After reading this book, you know the 10 questions you should ask to be ready to consider the purchase of a timeshare. With the answers to those questions, you should be armed with the knowledge to make the right decision for you.

If you have found this guide useful, please leave a positive review to help others avoid the pitfalls of the timeshare purchase process!

Thank you for reading "Timeshare Truths: 10 Essential Questions to secure Your Ideal Vacation Property."

We hope this book has shed light on the complicated world of timeshares, and would love to hear your thoughts on the information provided. Not only are your observations extremely helpful to us, but they are also quite valuable to potential buyers of timeshares who can gain from your experience.

We are especially interested in the following:

Application Value: Do you feel you now have the knowledge to better evaluate timeshares? Do you feel more confidence in your ability to make judgments based on this information?

Recommendation Factor: If you had friends or family members who were interest in timeshares, would you suggest this book to them based on your own experience?

New Understand or Surprises: In the book did you find any particular piece of advice that stood out or changed the way you view the ownership of a timeshare?

Your review can make a difference. By sharing your review, you're helping others to wade through the complex world of timeshares with a little more confidence. Your perspective can be a guiding light for someone else's decision-making process.

Please scan the QR code to leave your review:

Thank you for taking the time to share your valuable thoughts and experiences.

References

American Resort Development Association (ARDA). *US timeshare industry: By the numbers.* (n.d.). https://www.arda.org/news-communications/timeshare-industry-basics/us-timeshare-industry-numbers

Araj, V. (2022, October 25). *What is a timeshare and is it worth buying?* QuickenLoans. https://www.quickenloans.com/learn/what-is-a-timeshare

Bennett, K. (2022, November 29). *The average cost of a vacation: Transportation, food, entertainment and more.* Bankrate. https://www.bankrate.com/banking/cost-of-vacation/#budget-tips

Centerstone Group. *Timeshare price.* (n.d.). https://centerstonegroup.com/timeshare-cost/

Finn Law Group. *Some stunning statistics about timeshare rescission.* (n.d.). https://finnlawgroup.com/statistics-about-timeshare-rescission/

Jade. (2022, May 17). *US vacation rental rates: Most expensive US markets in 2022.* Transparent. https://seetransparent.com/blog/us-vacation-rental-rates-most-expensive-us-markets-in-2022/ accessed 12/01/23

MyTimeshareExitReviews.com. *Why timeshares lose value.* (n.d.). https://www.mytimeshareexitreviews.com/why-timeshares-lose-value/

Spaulding Jr., A. O., Dennison, K. D., & Freedman, R. S. (2022). *Federal and state regulation of timeshares and fractional interests.* Issuu. https://issuu.com/rptelaw/docs/2022-aba-rpte-v36-03-may-june-issue/s/15636544

Made in the USA
Monee, IL
07 November 2026

68012409R10030